Things Never to Tell Children

The School of Life

After a long and happy childhood, one day, Bunny's parents told him that it was time for him to go out and explore the wonders and beauty of the world...

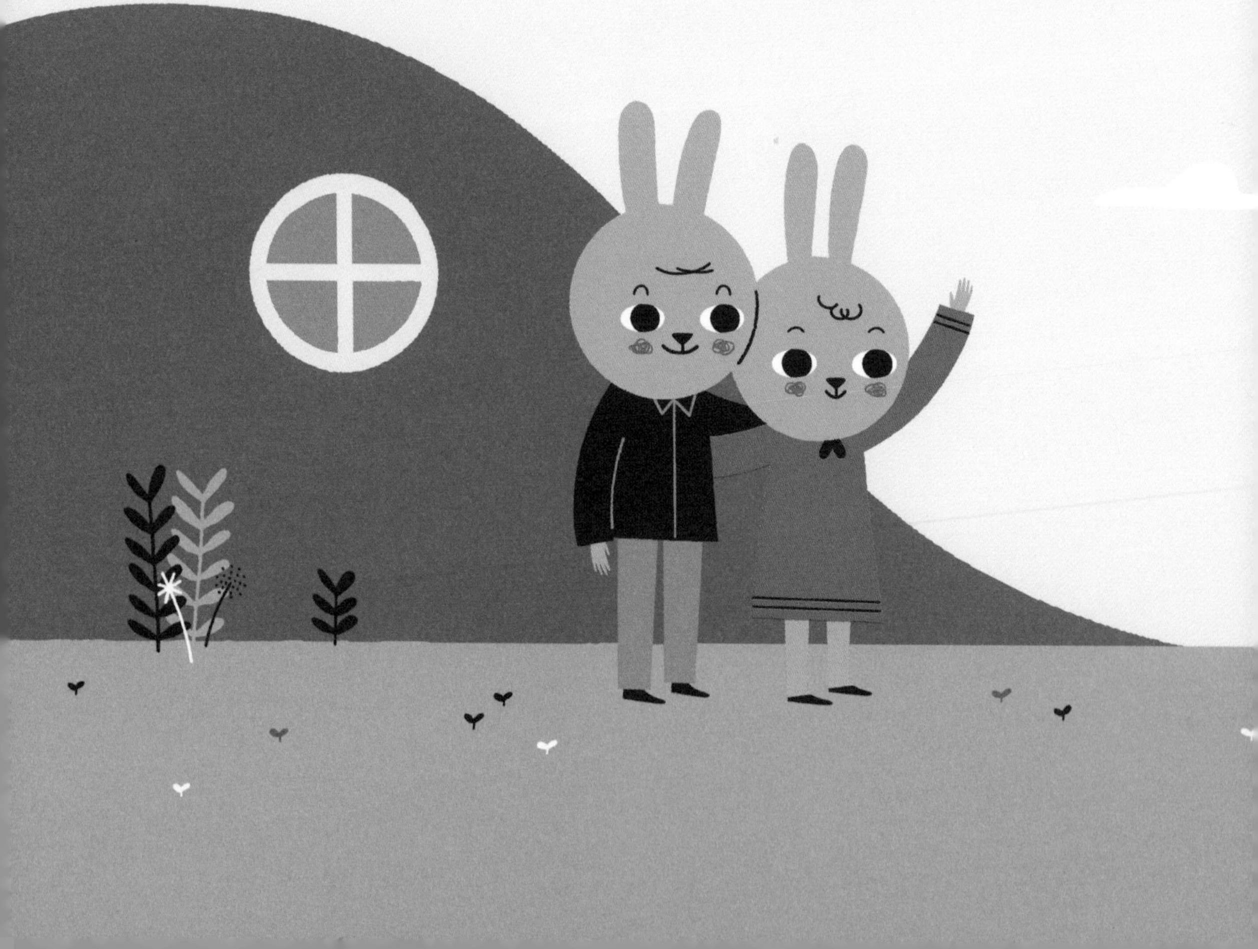

...to survive without their assistance, pay for everything himself and solve his problems on his own.

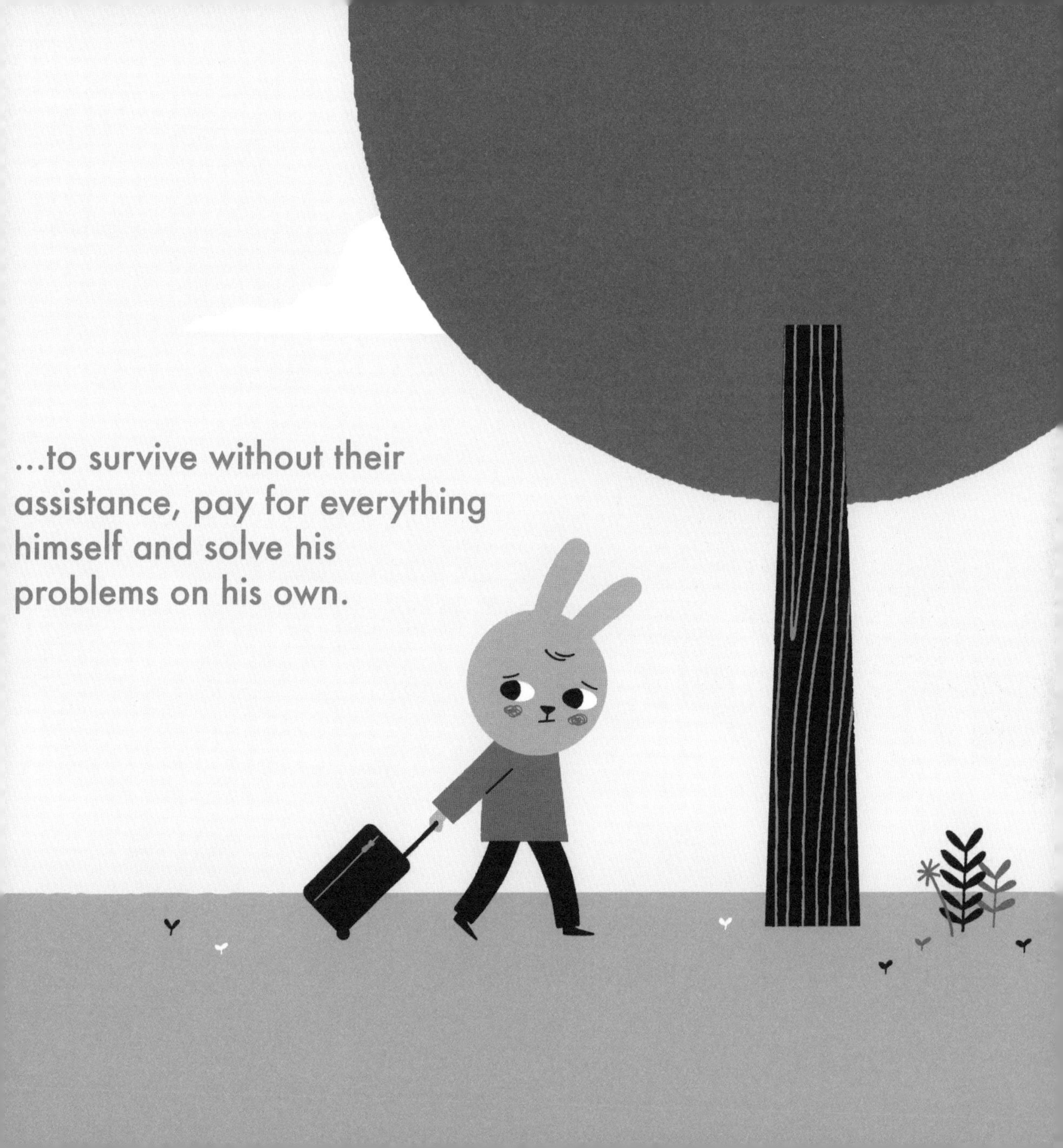

Bunny looked for work that would give him meaning and make a difference to the lives of others...

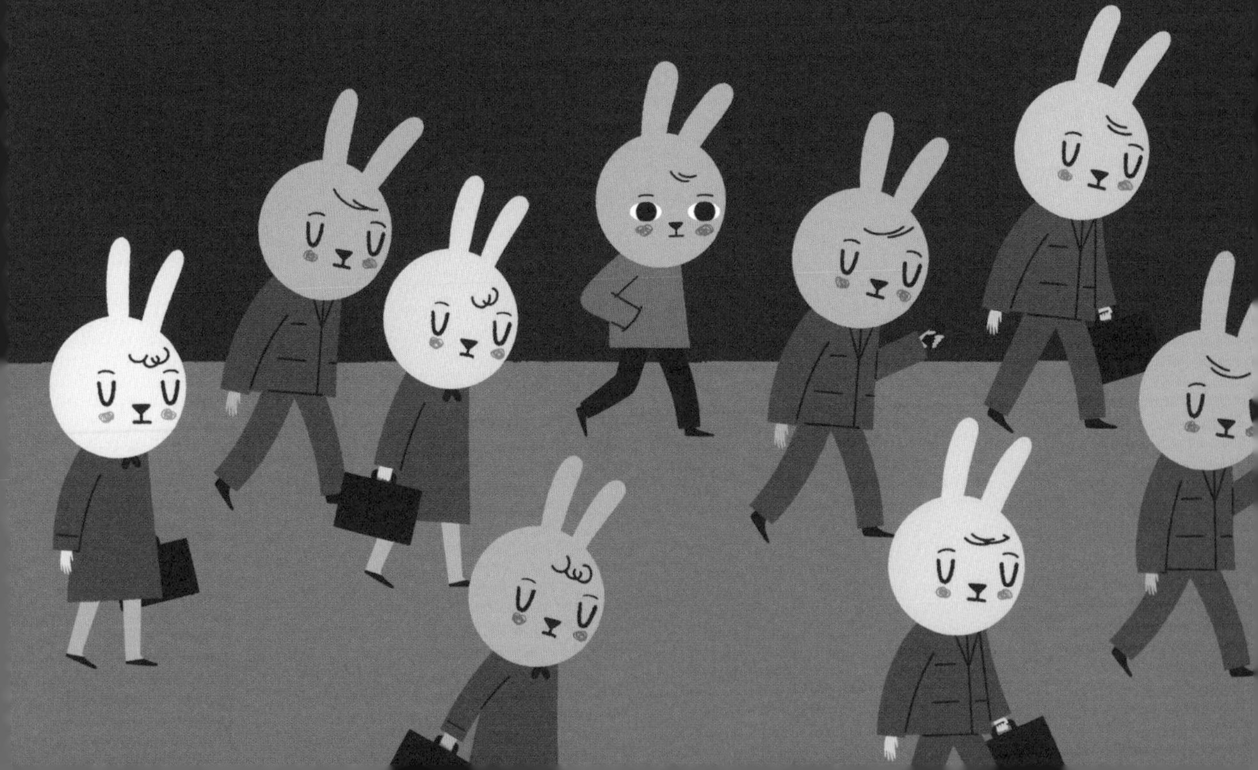

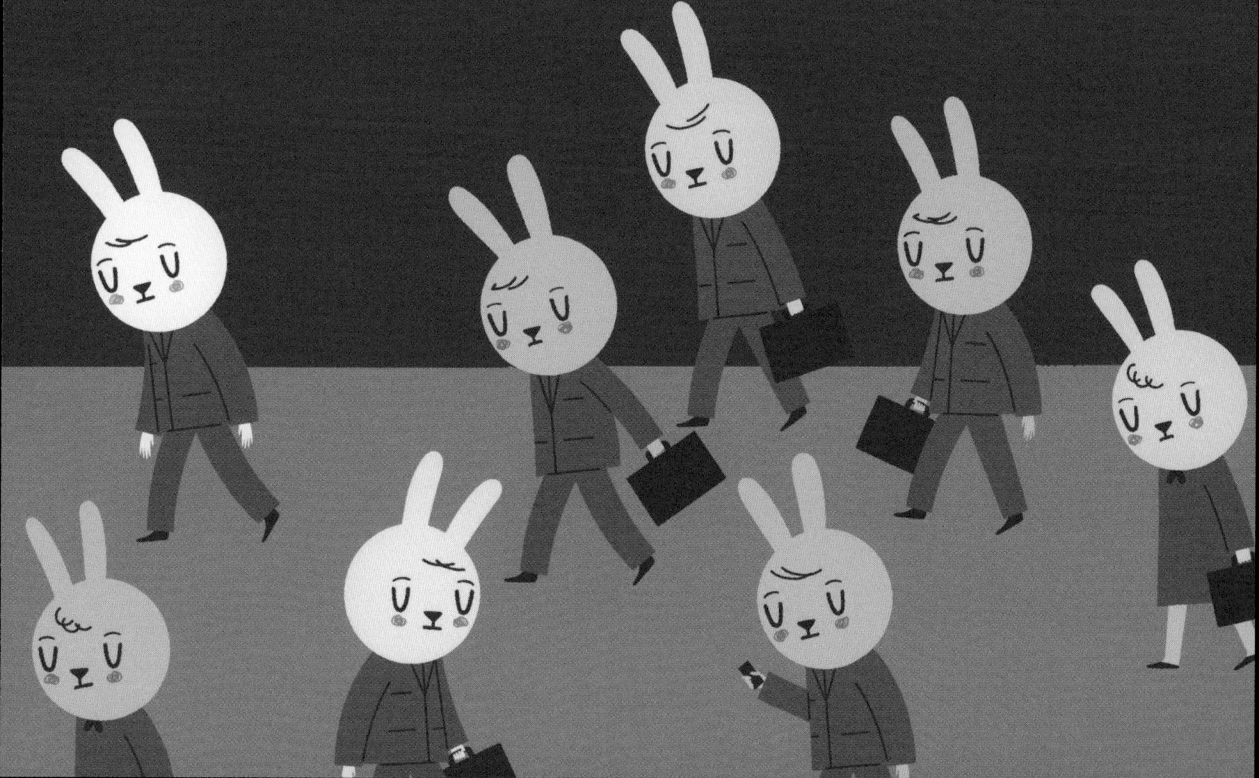

Bunny longed to love someone who would understand him entirely and with whose soul his own could fuse.

Mostly though, he looked at photographs of other rabbits and afterwards felt everything pure and good within him had died.

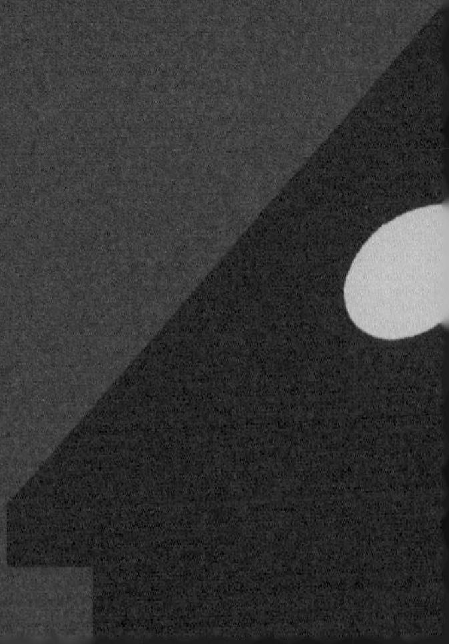

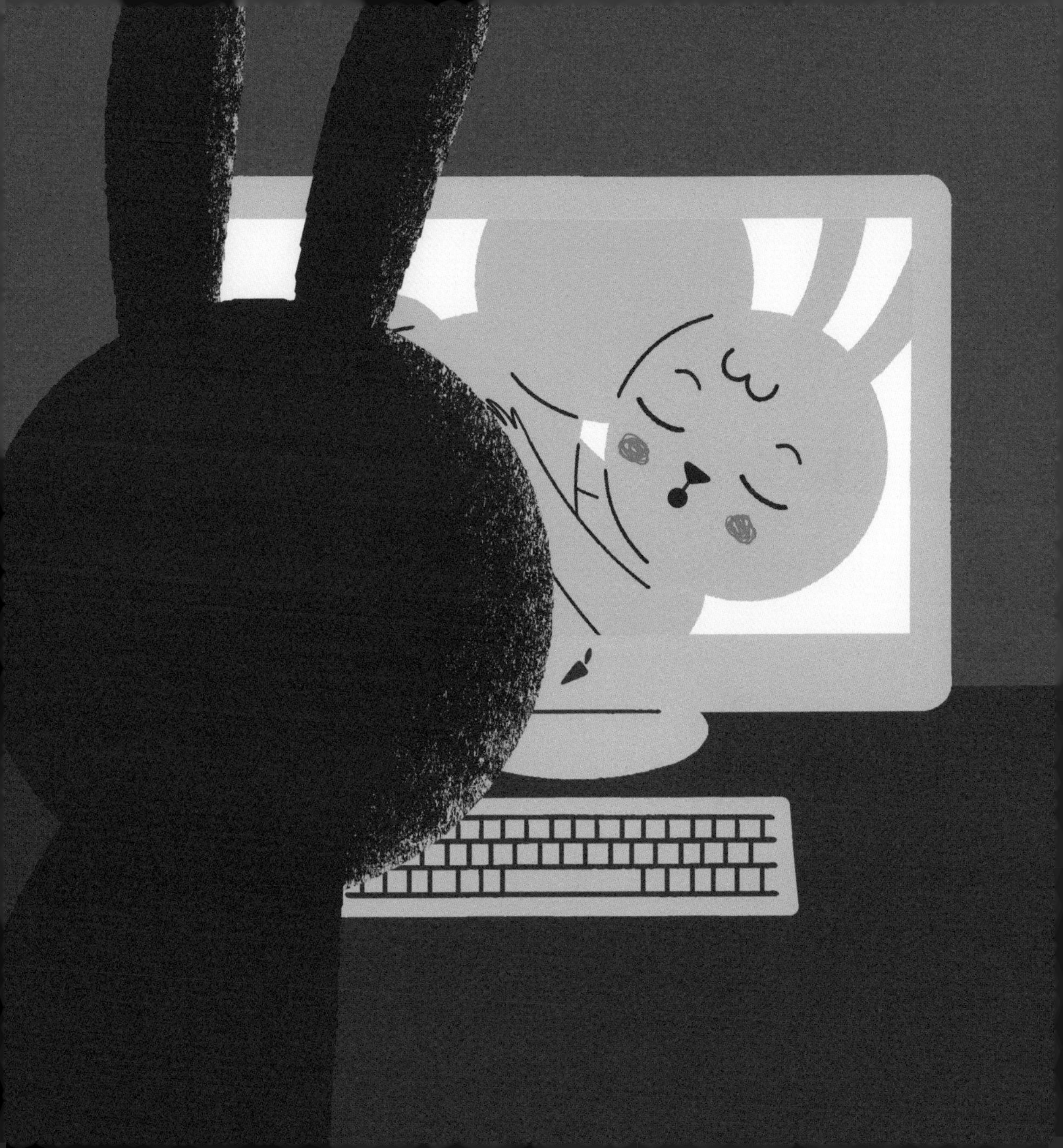

Bunny had several friends with whom
he liked to go out for a drink...

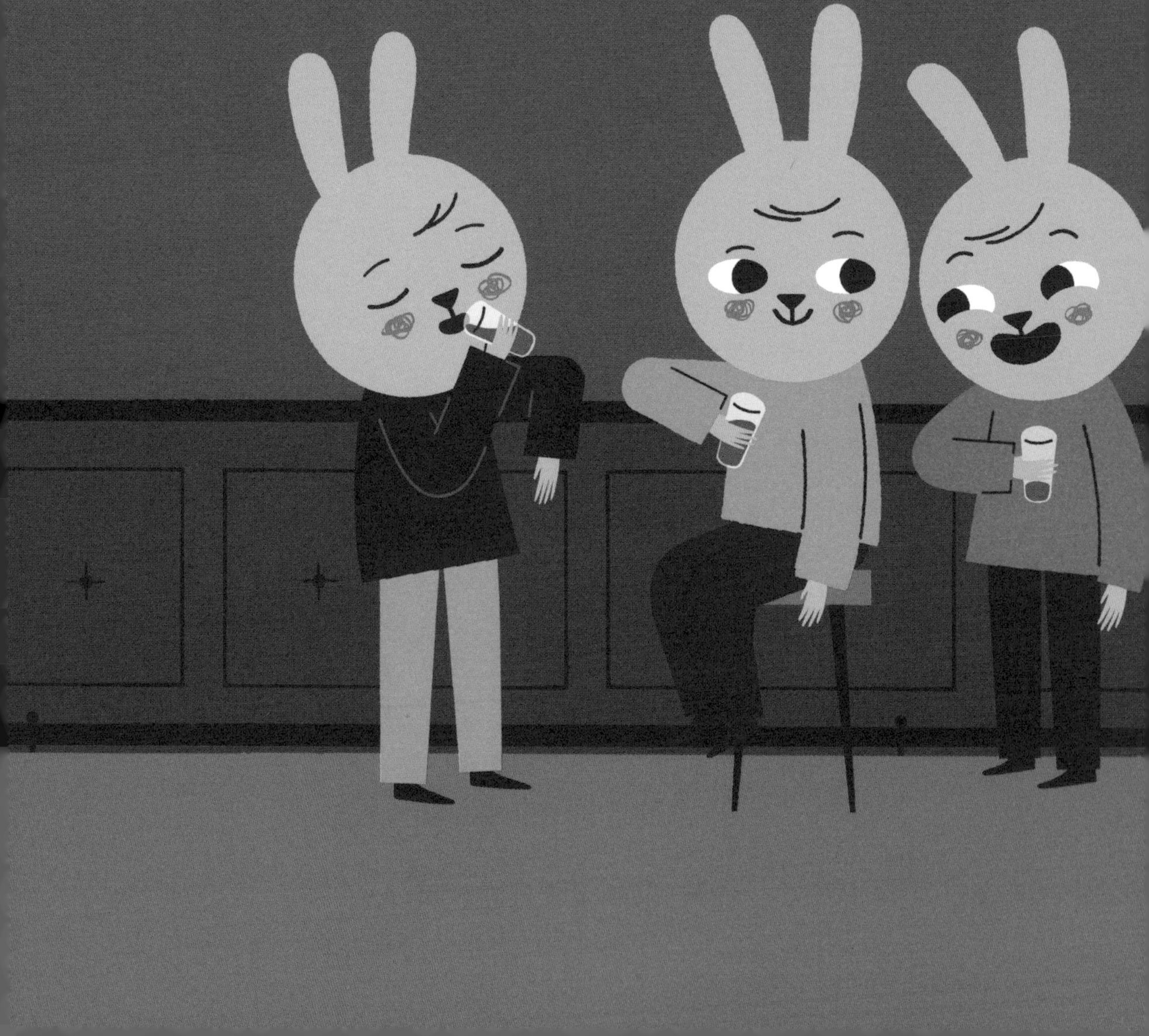

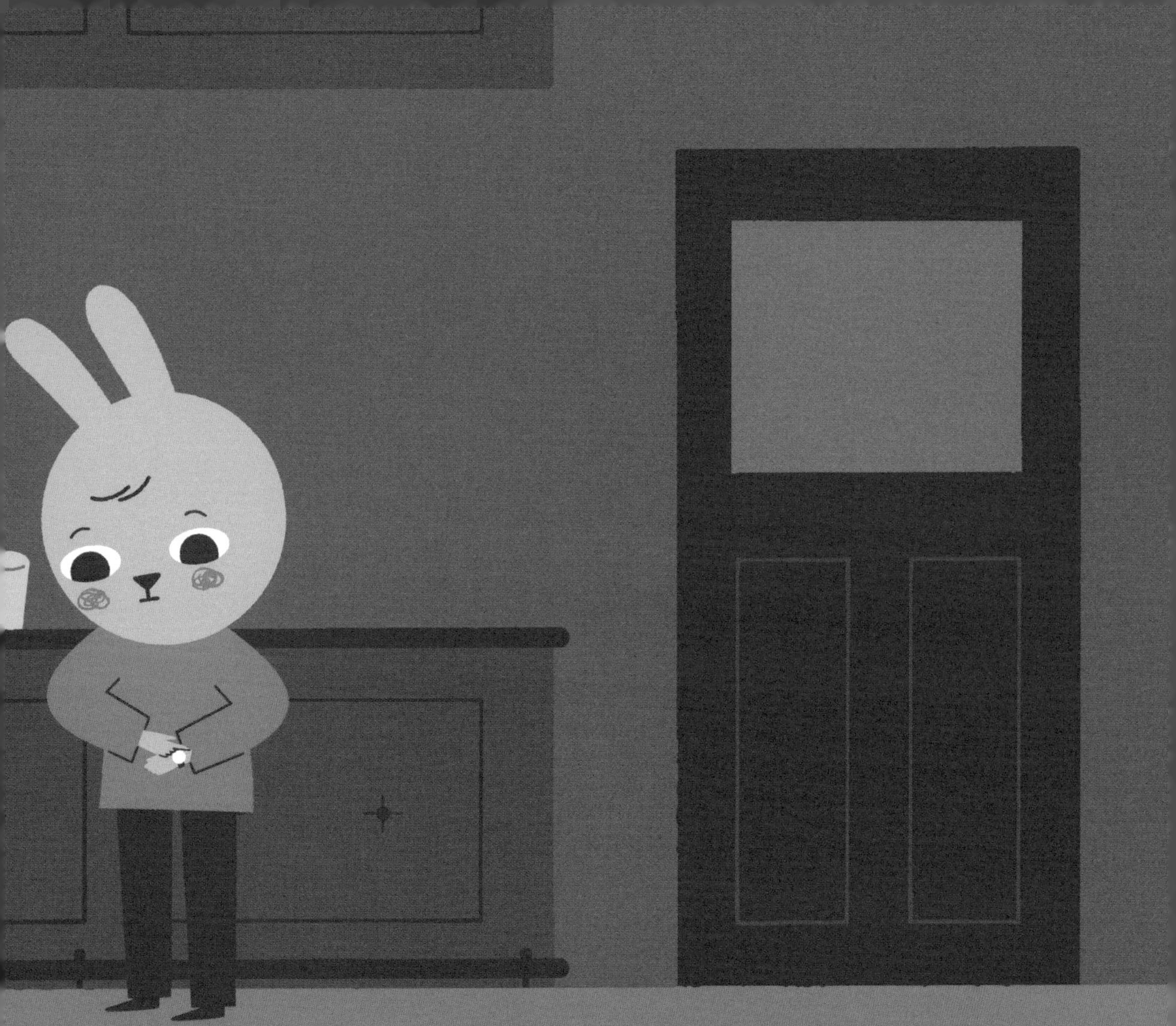

...and for a few hours, drown the knowledge that he would have to die unlamented and irredeemably alone in a pitiless universe.

Sometimes, Bunny longed to believe in a giant rabbit in the sky who would look upon his failings and follies with generosity.

It turned out that the laws of science had proved there couldn't be such a rabbit.

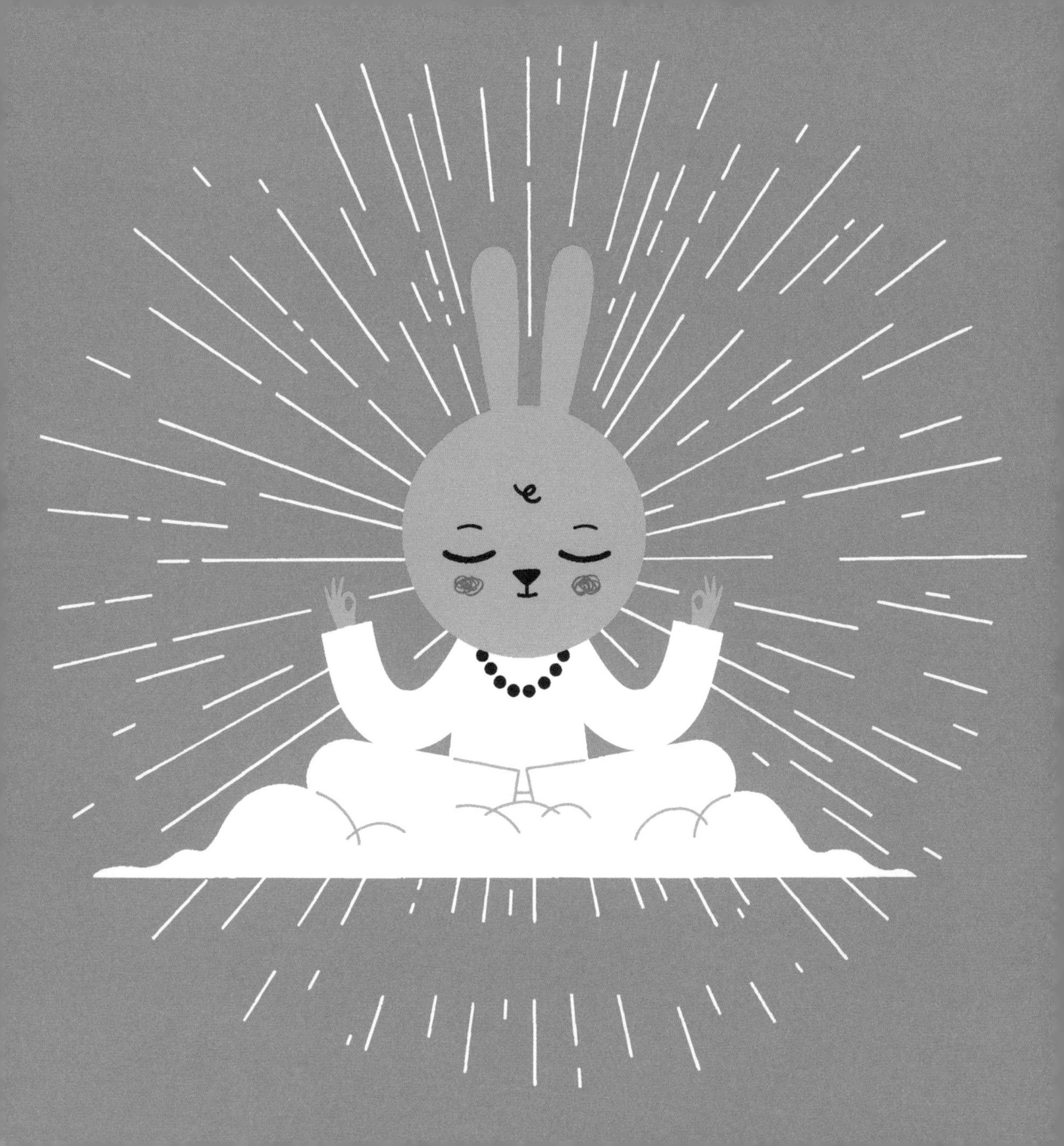

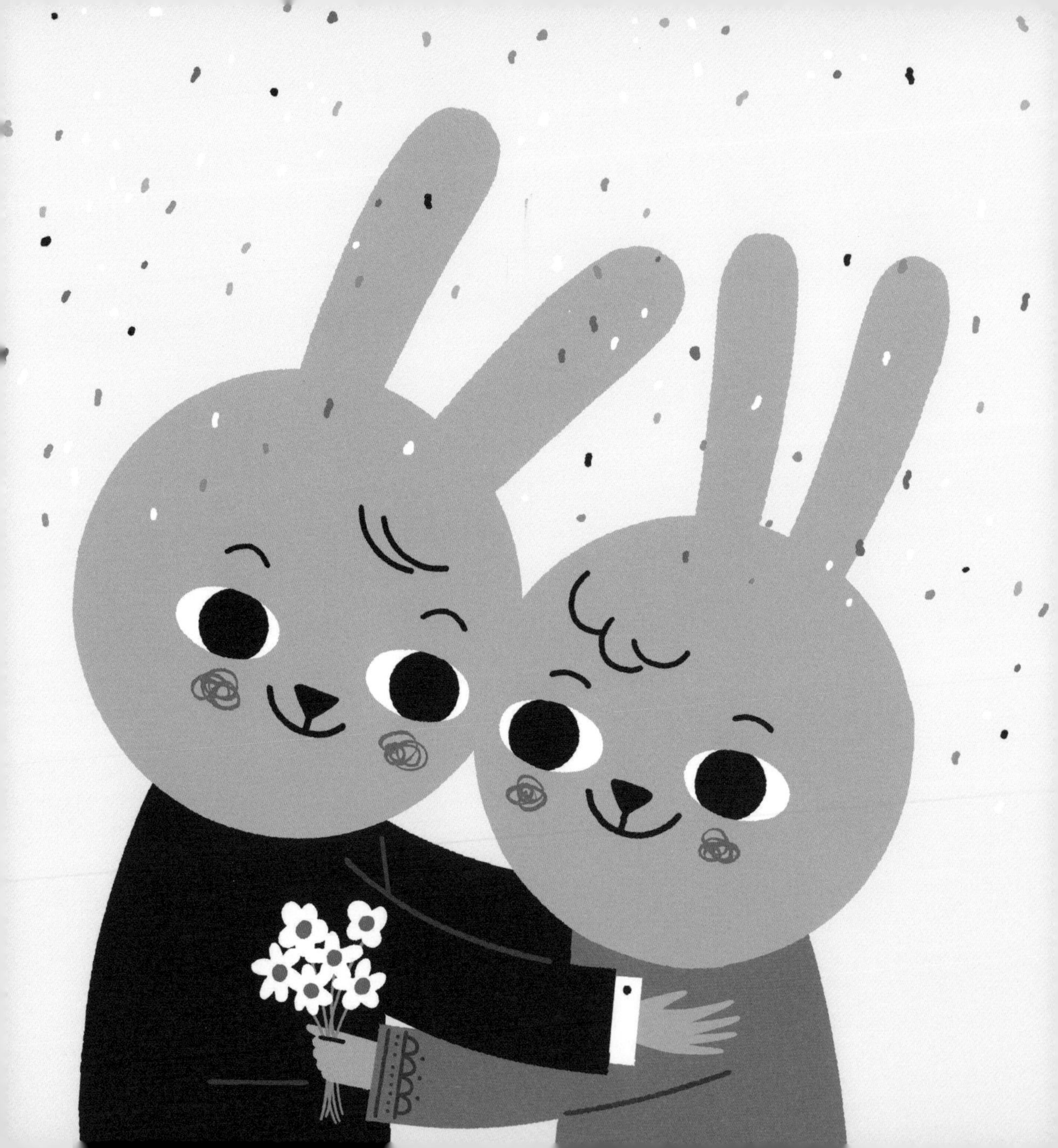

Bunny got married.

He hated the feeling of being
alone slightly more than he loved
the rabbit he'd proposed to.

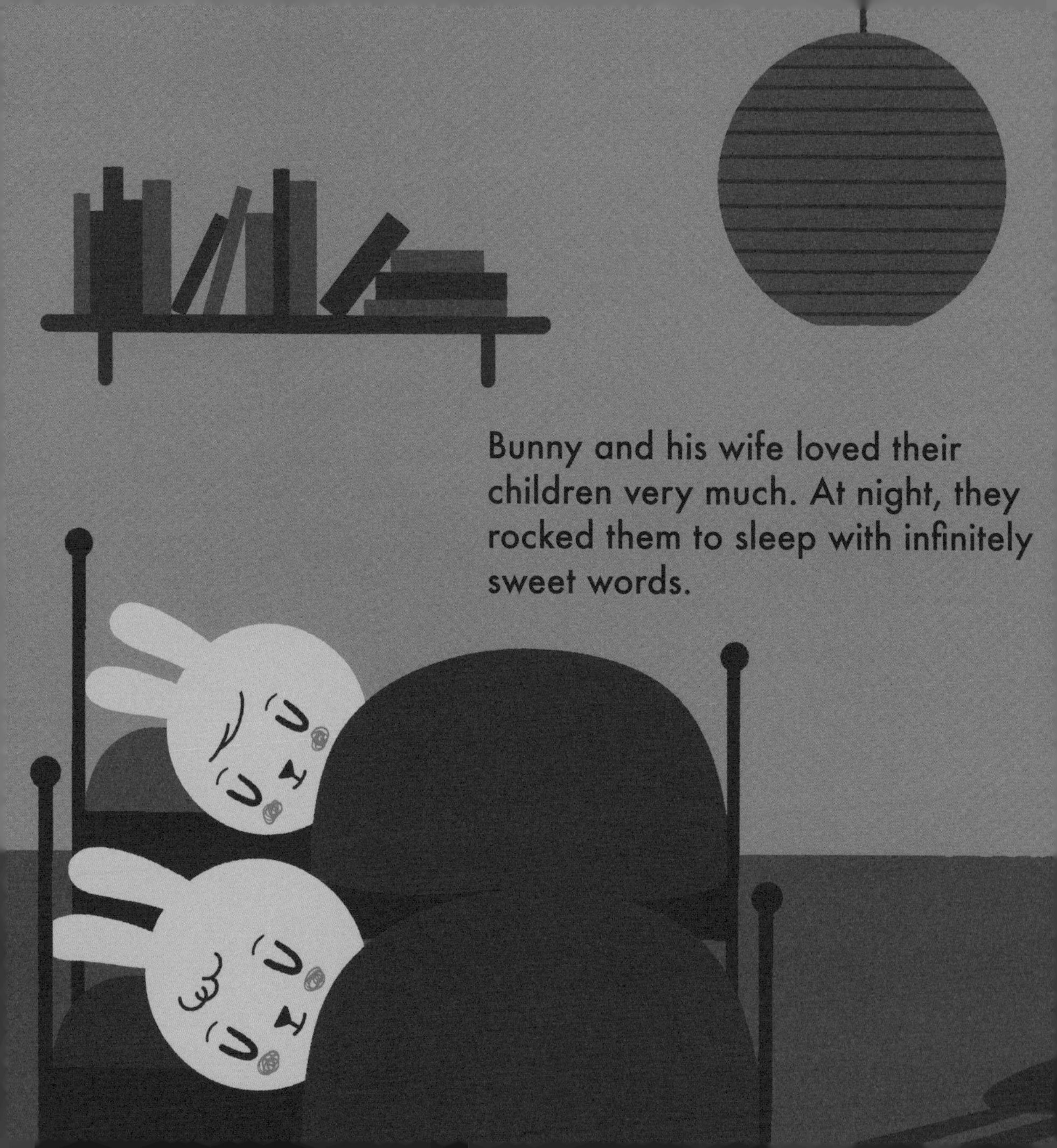

Bunny and his wife loved their children very much. At night, they rocked them to sleep with infinitely sweet words.

And afterwards, referred to each other with vicious names like carrot-face and arse-ears.

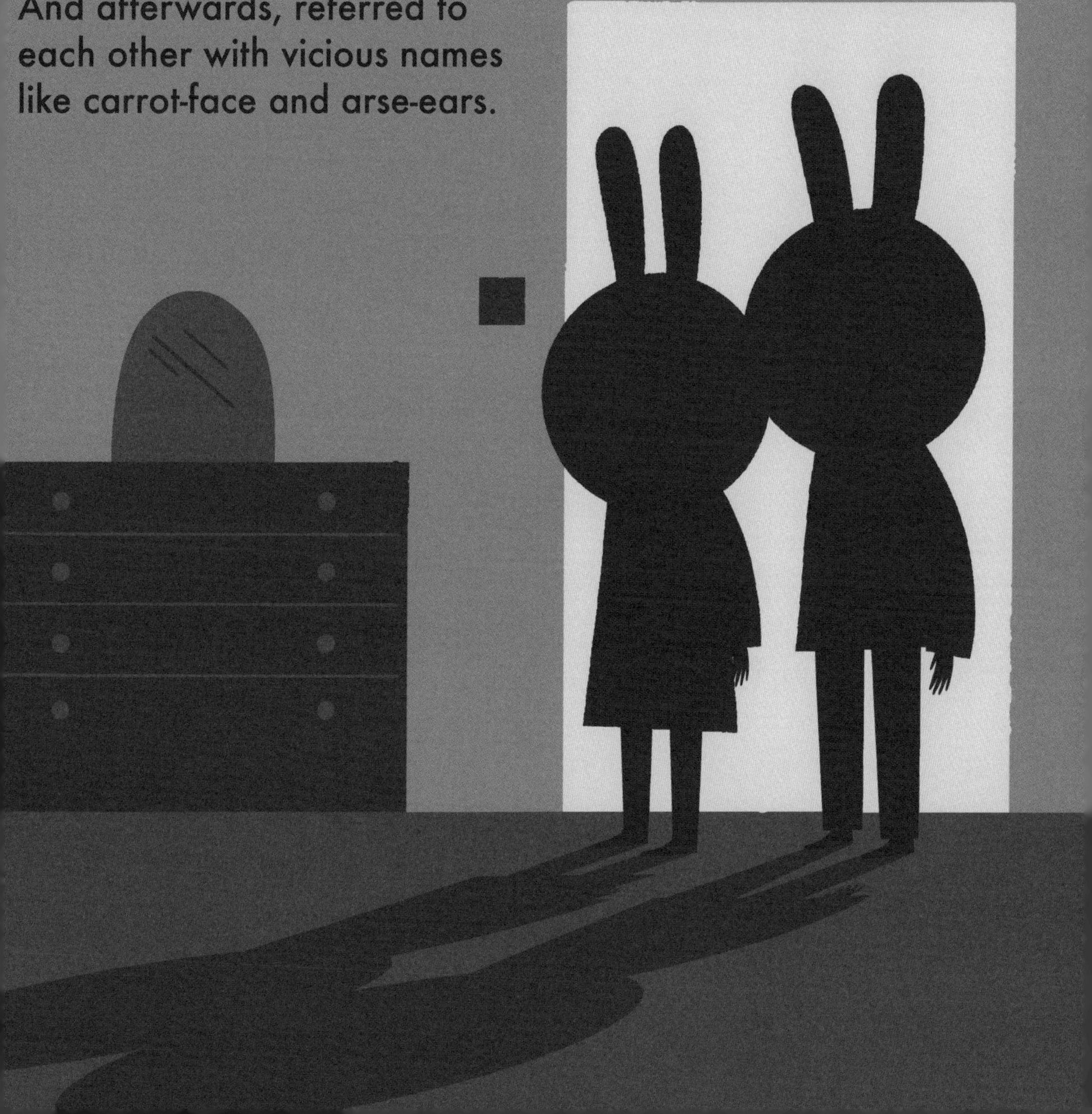

While brushing his teeth,
Bunny sometimes thought briefly...

...that it might be nice
simply not to exist.

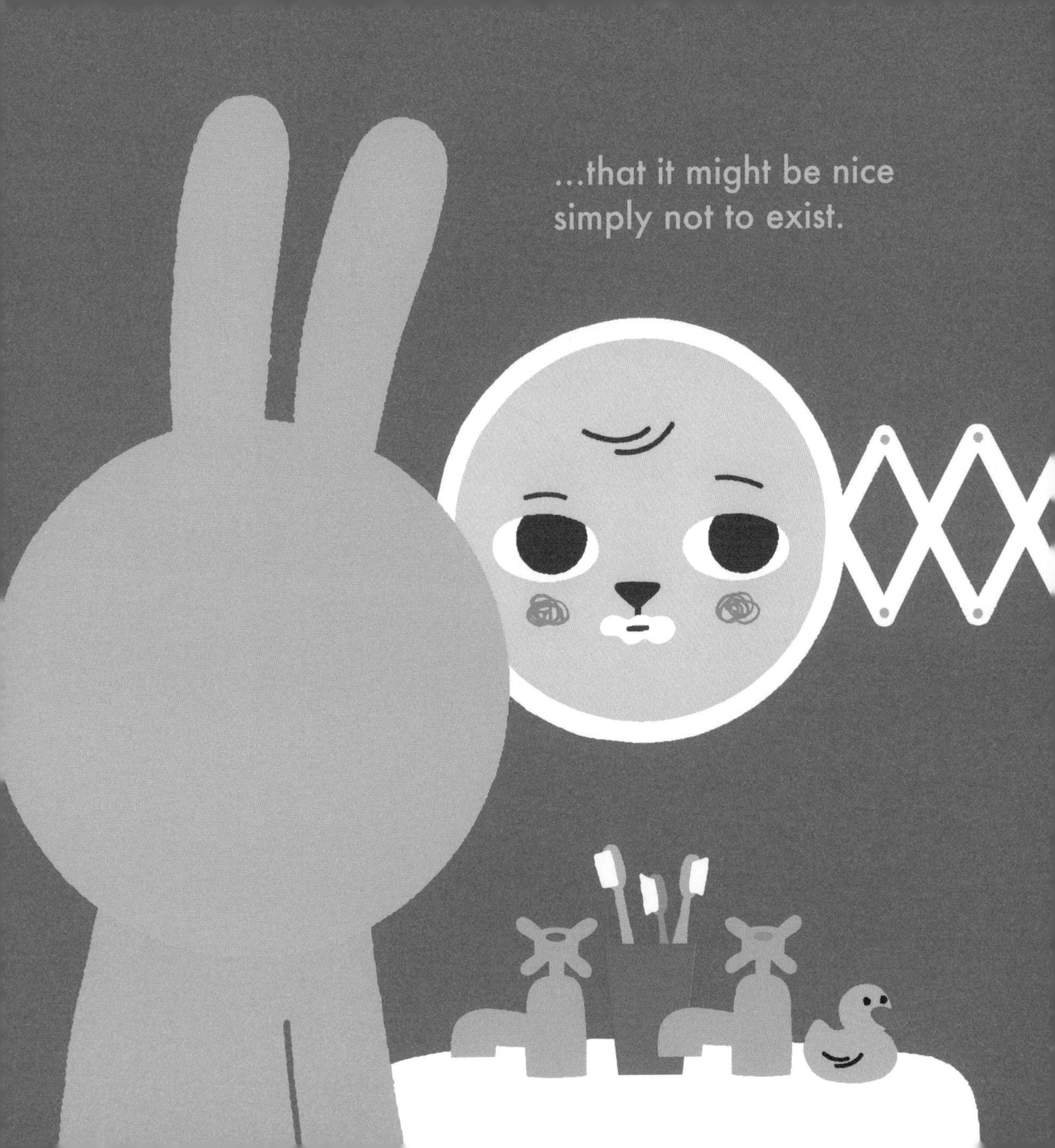

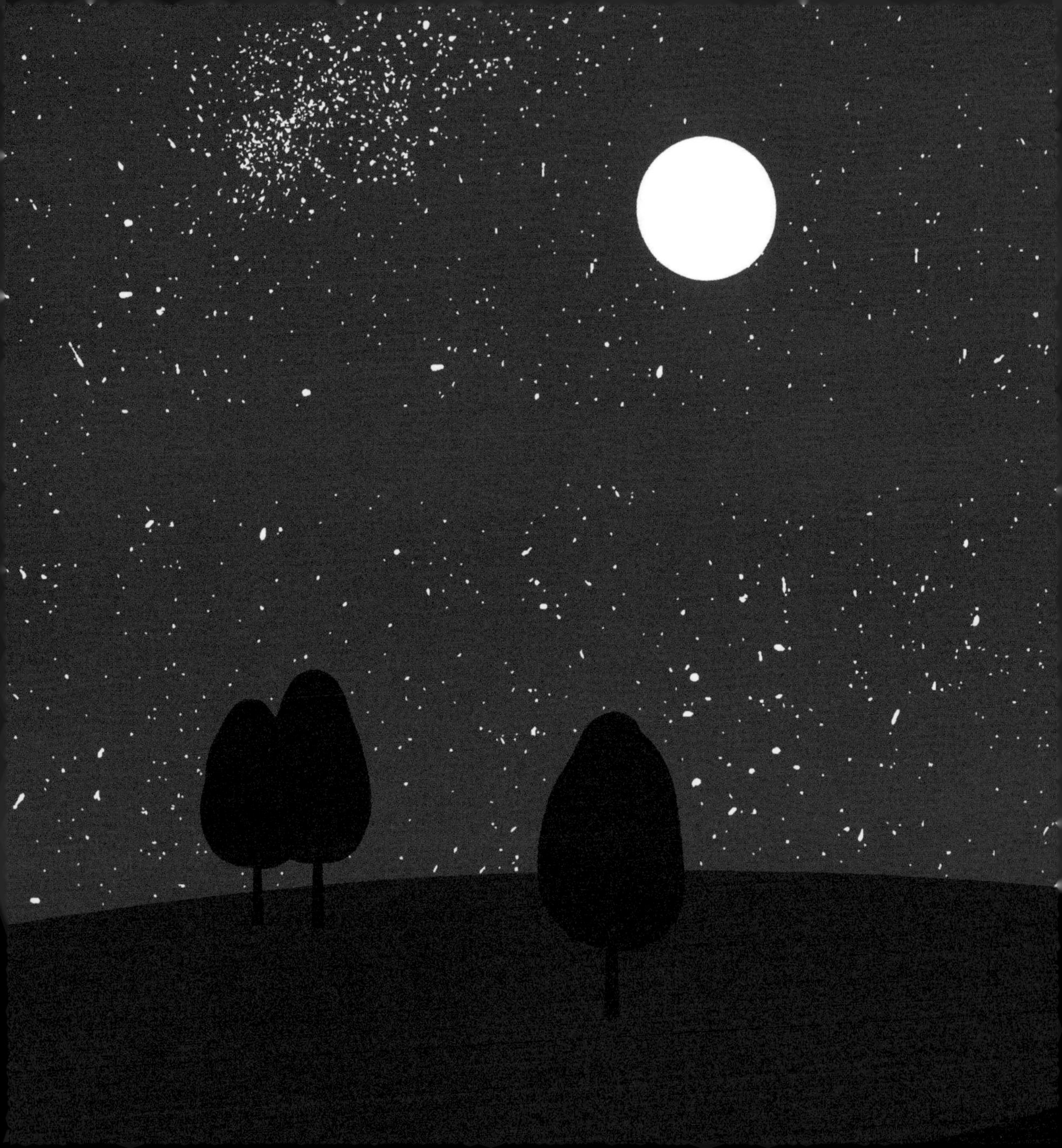

Bunny looked up at the sky: vast, majestic and eternal. He felt very small and very big at the same time – and longed for there to be someone to share the feeling with.

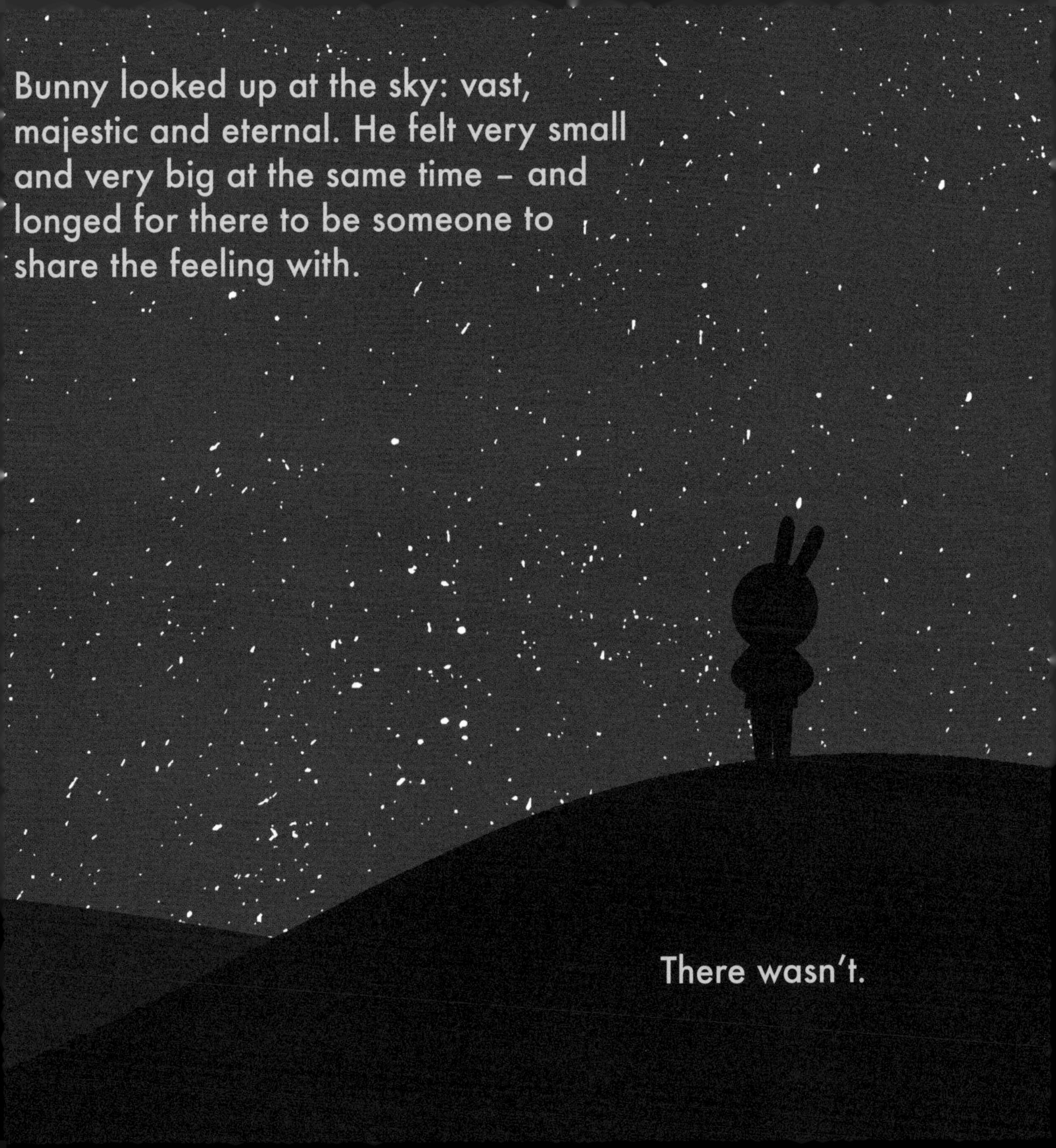

There wasn't.

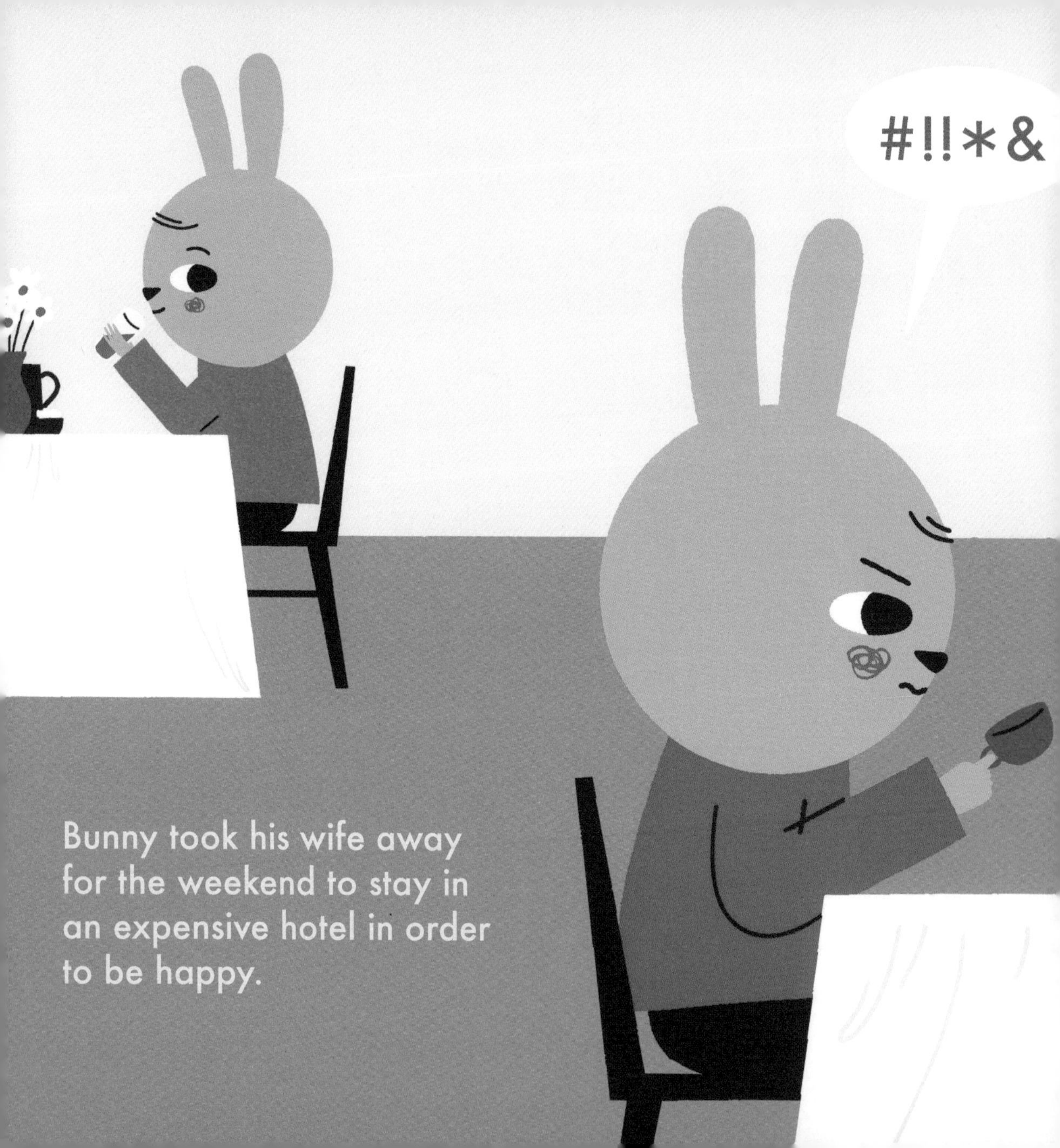
#!!*&

Bunny took his wife away for the weekend to stay in an expensive hotel in order to be happy.

At breakfast, they argued violently in a way that made other rabbits in the hotel feel very awkward...

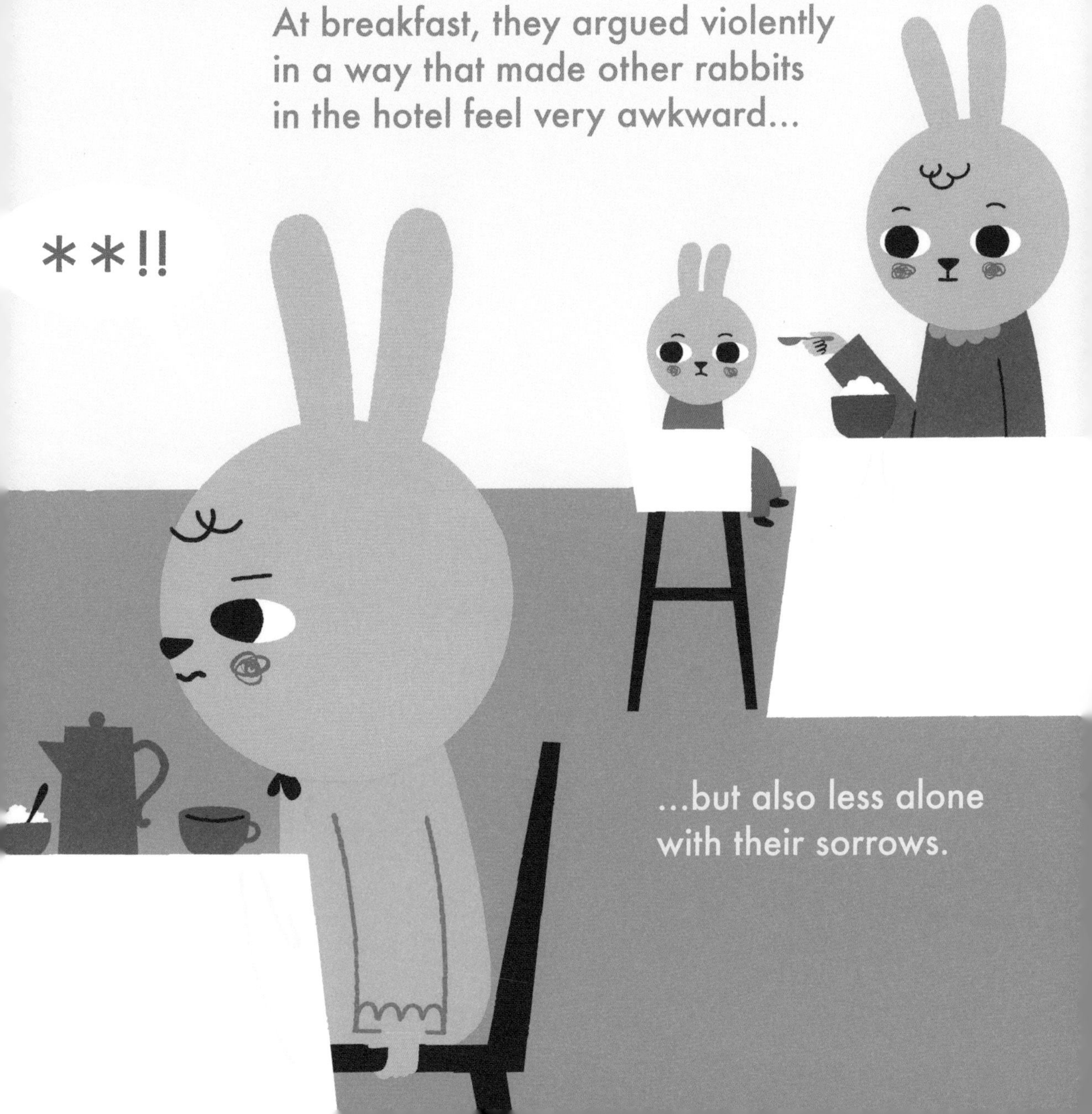
**!!

...but also less alone with their sorrows.

Bunny grew unable to sleep.

It was his mind's revenge for all the sad thoughts he had tried so hard not to have in the day.

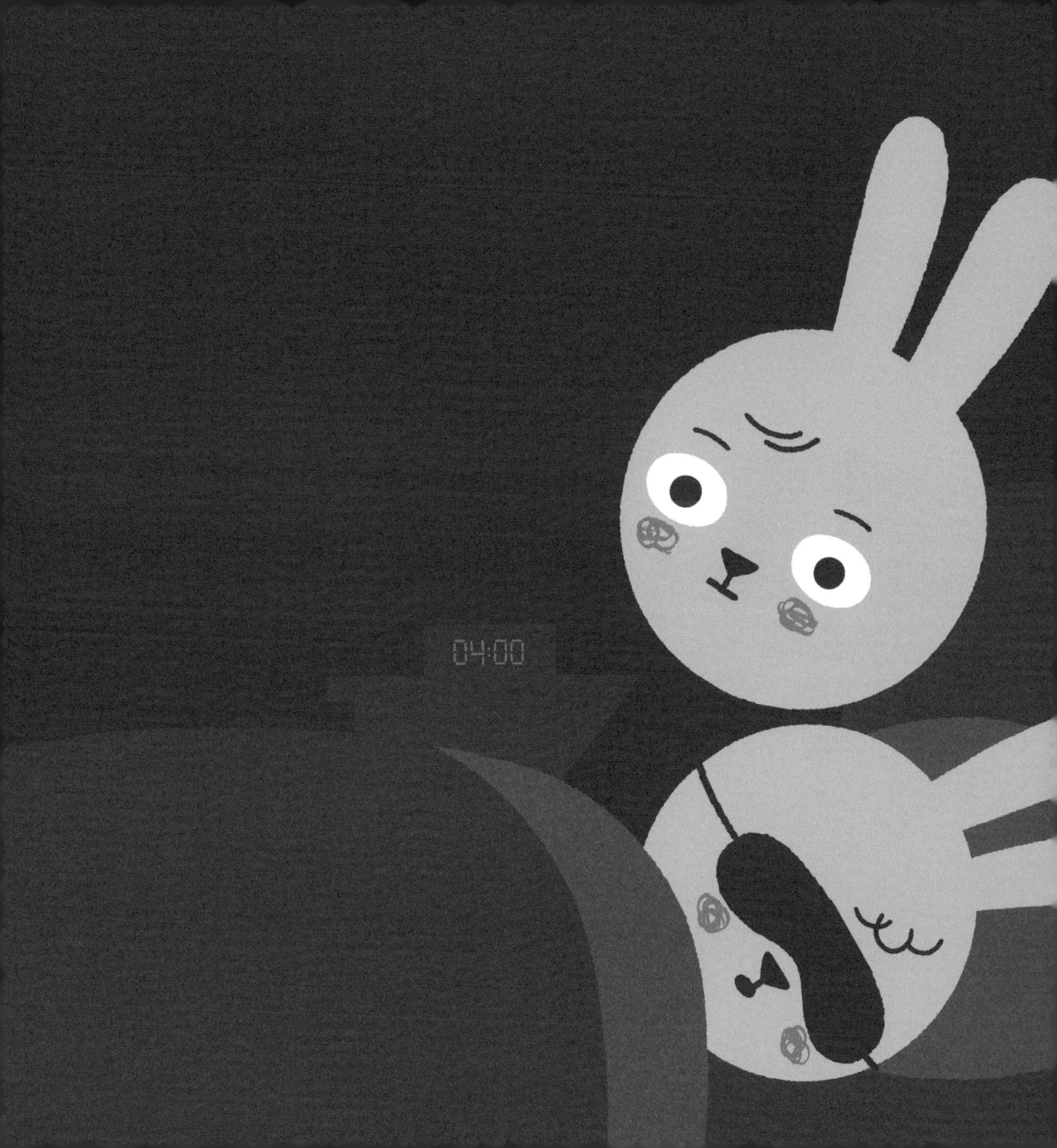
04:00

Bunny wondered if he had been singled out for unusual punishment or if his life was, in the structure of its disenchantments, essentially normal.

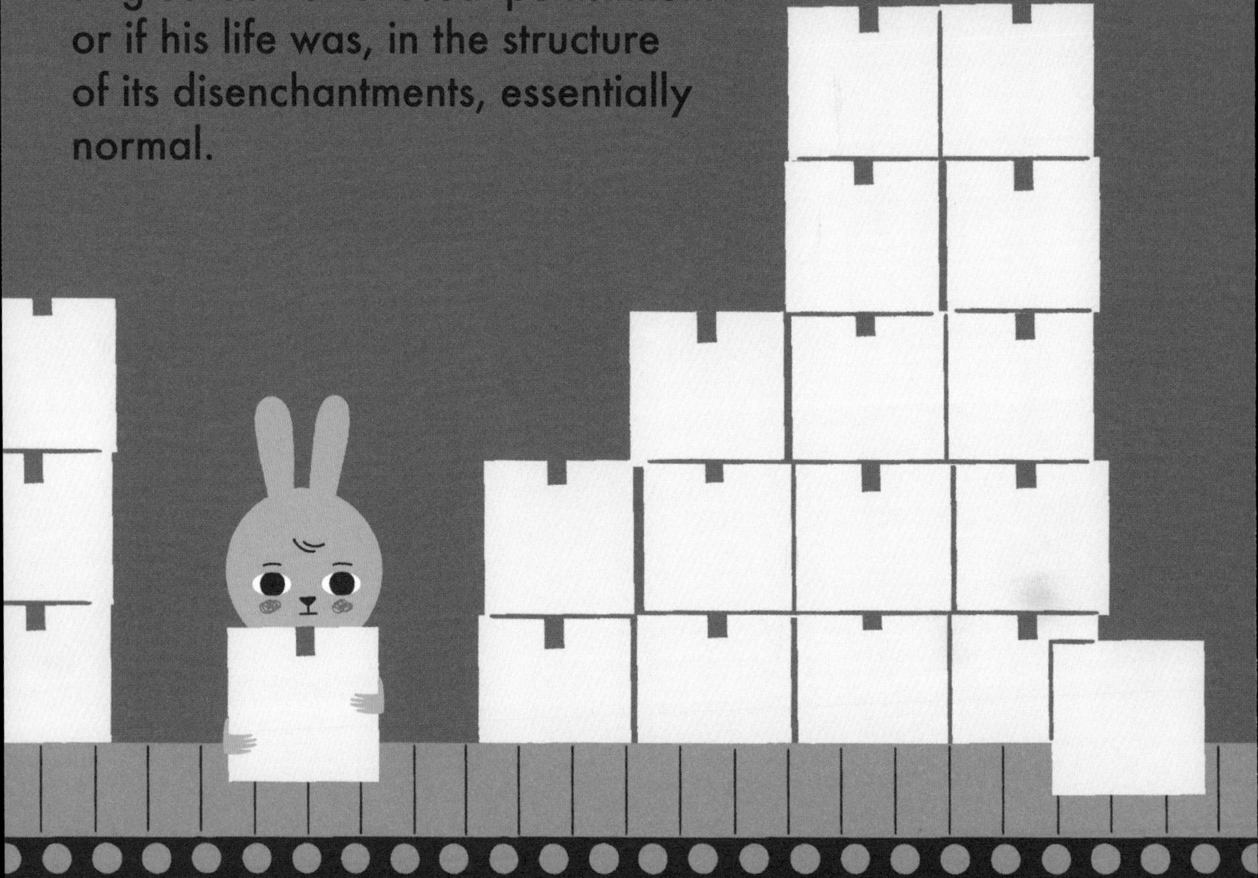

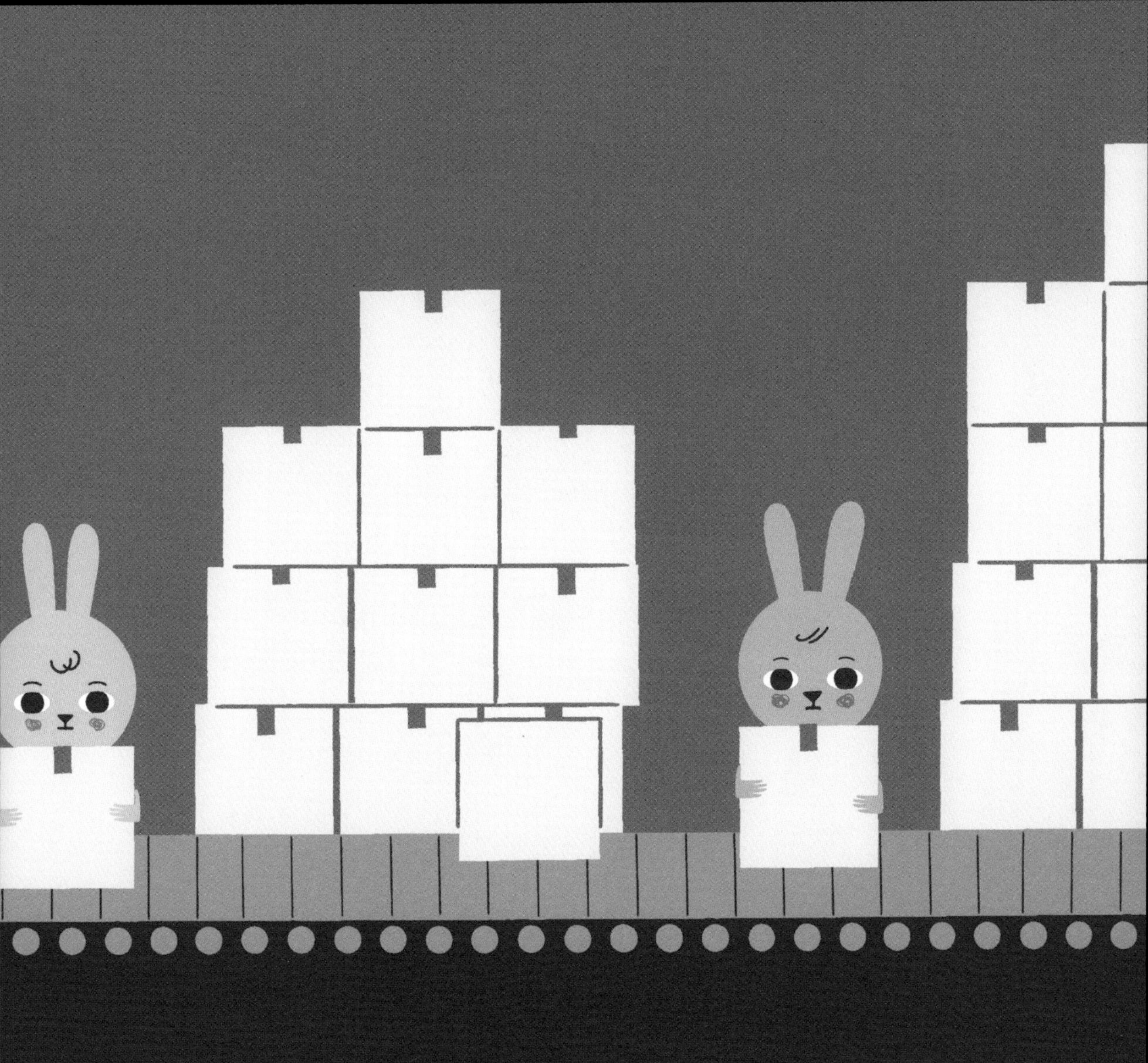

It was normal.

Bunny's acquaintances seemed
outwardly jolly and upbeat.
He wondered if they were masking
their griefs beneath a surface
sentimental cheeriness.

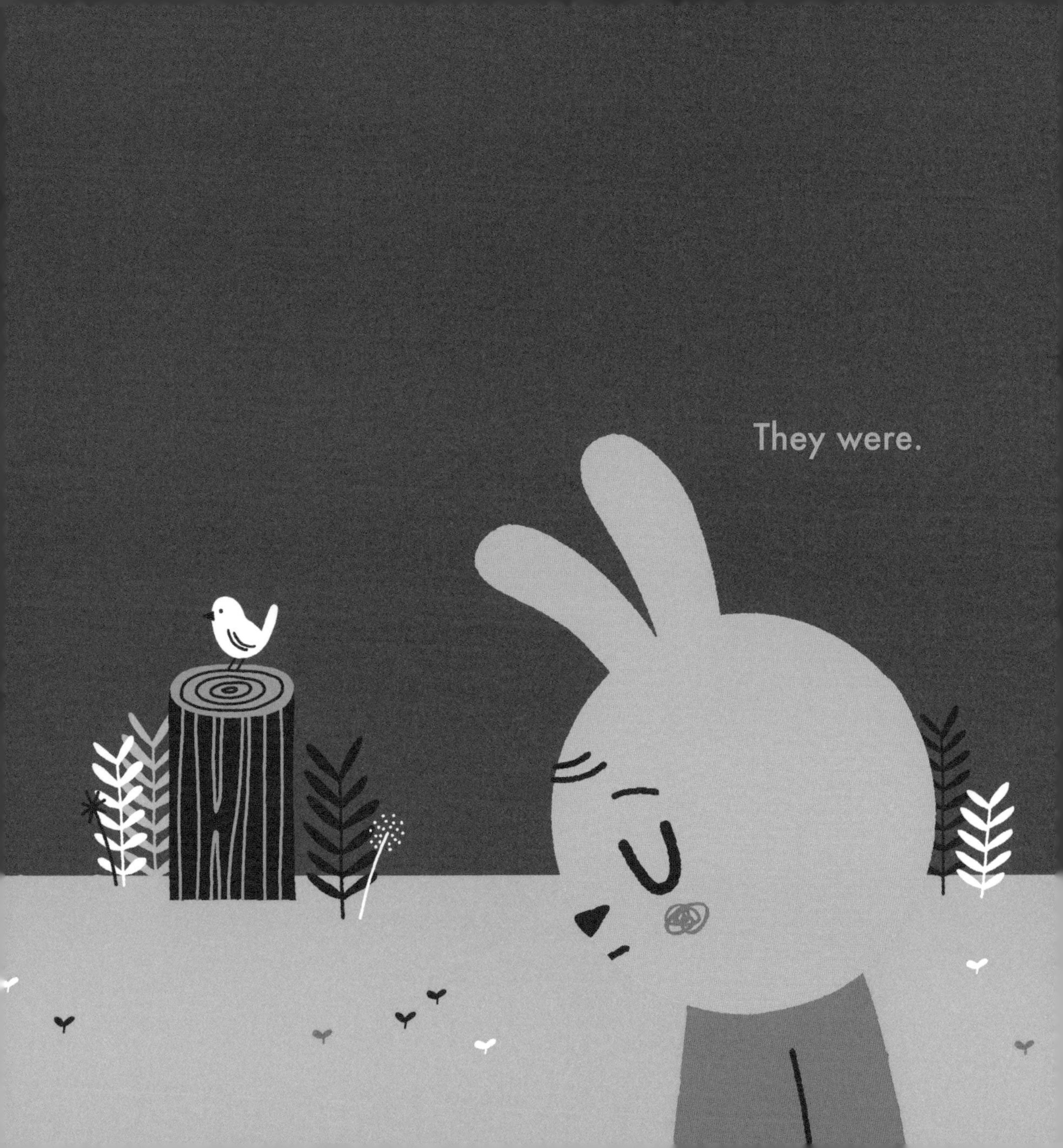

They were.

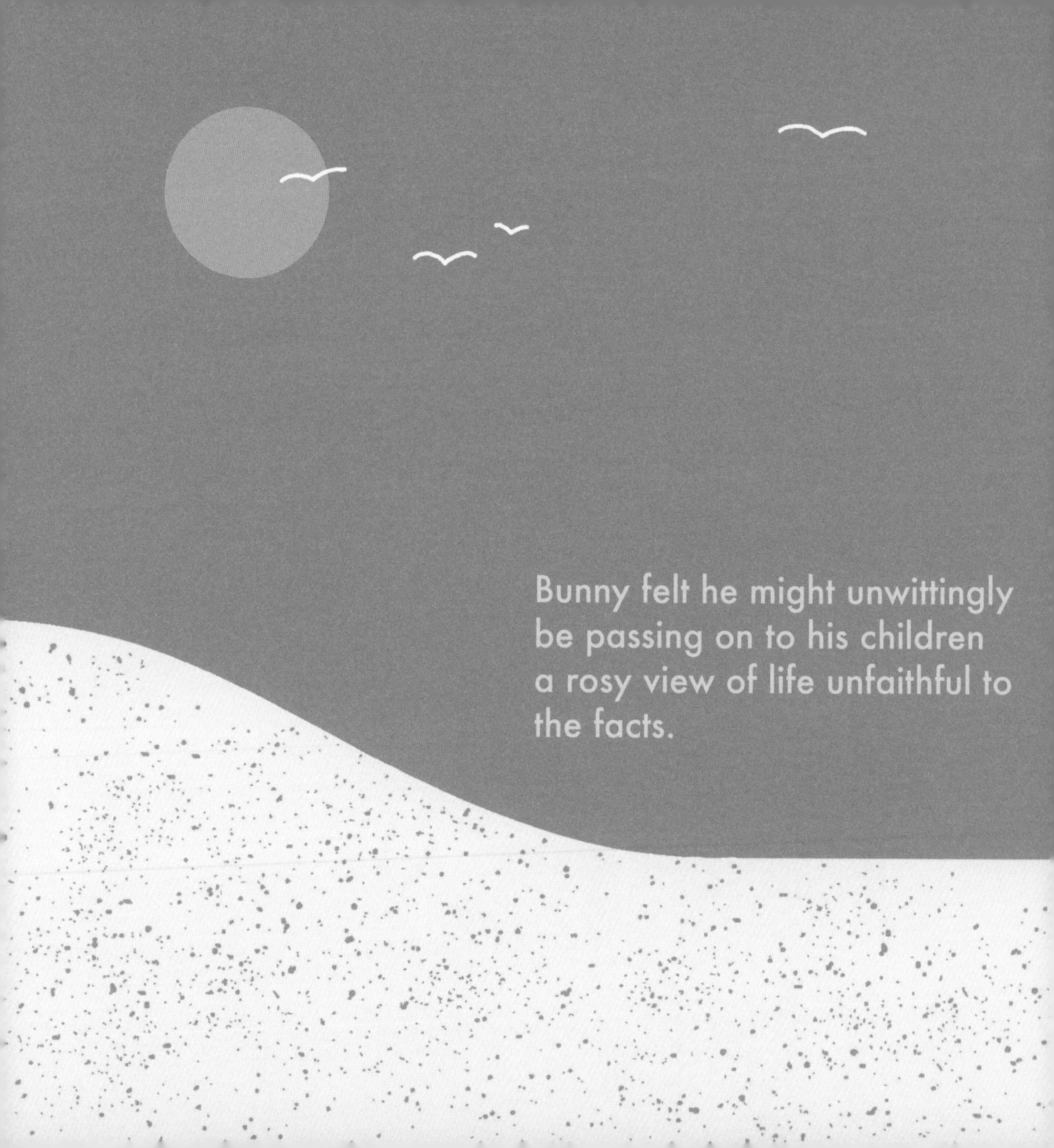

Bunny felt he might unwittingly be passing on to his children a rosy view of life unfaithful to the facts.

He was.

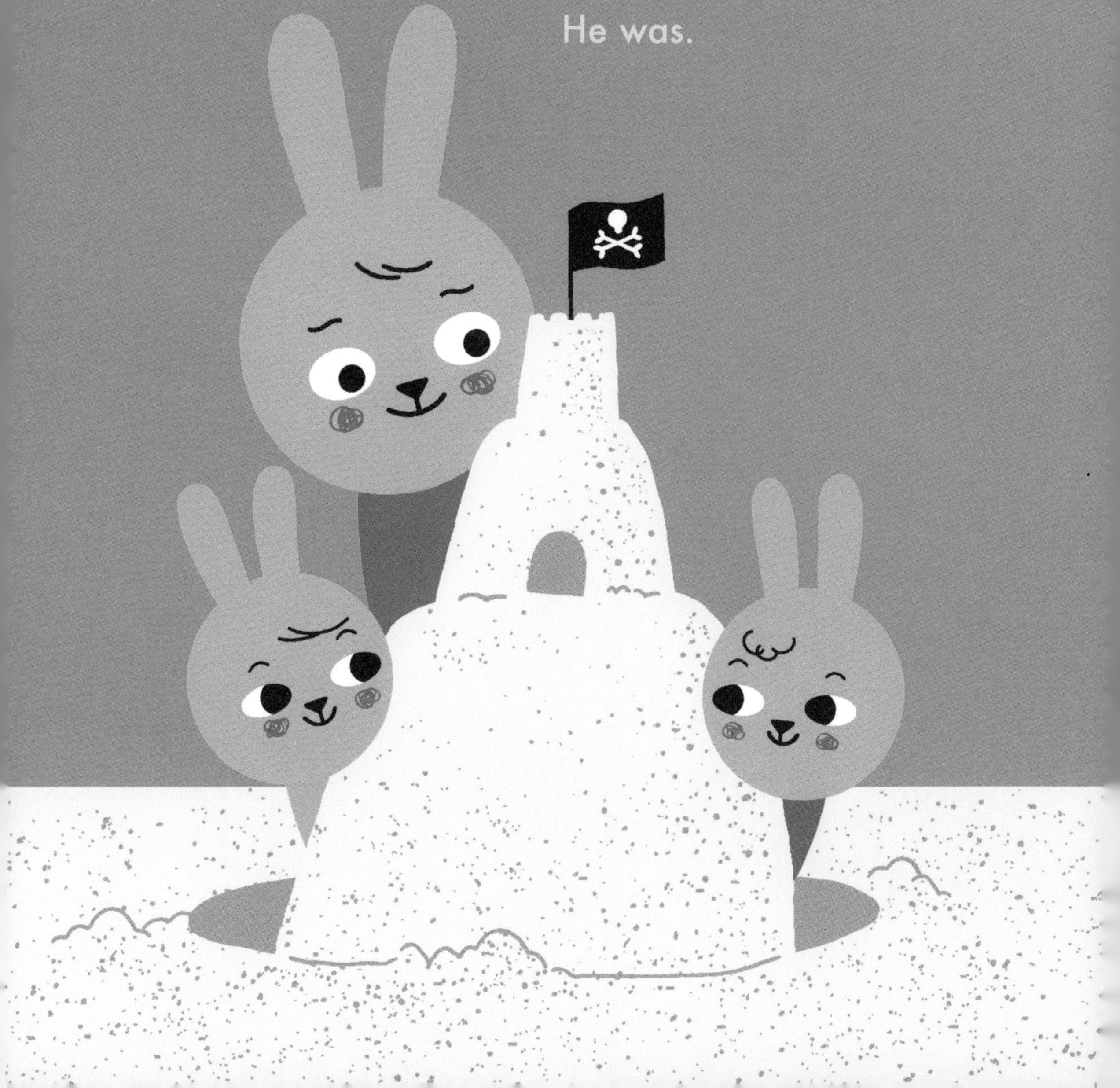

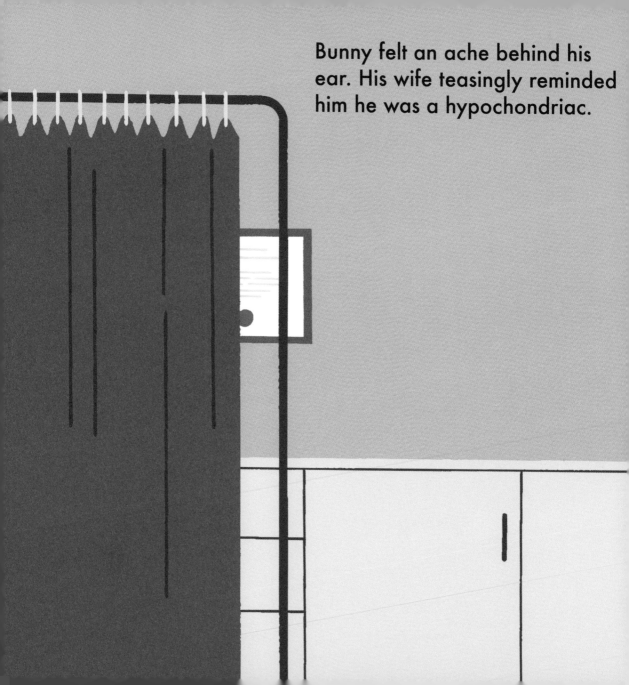

Bunny felt an ache behind his ear. His wife teasingly reminded him he was a hypochondriac.

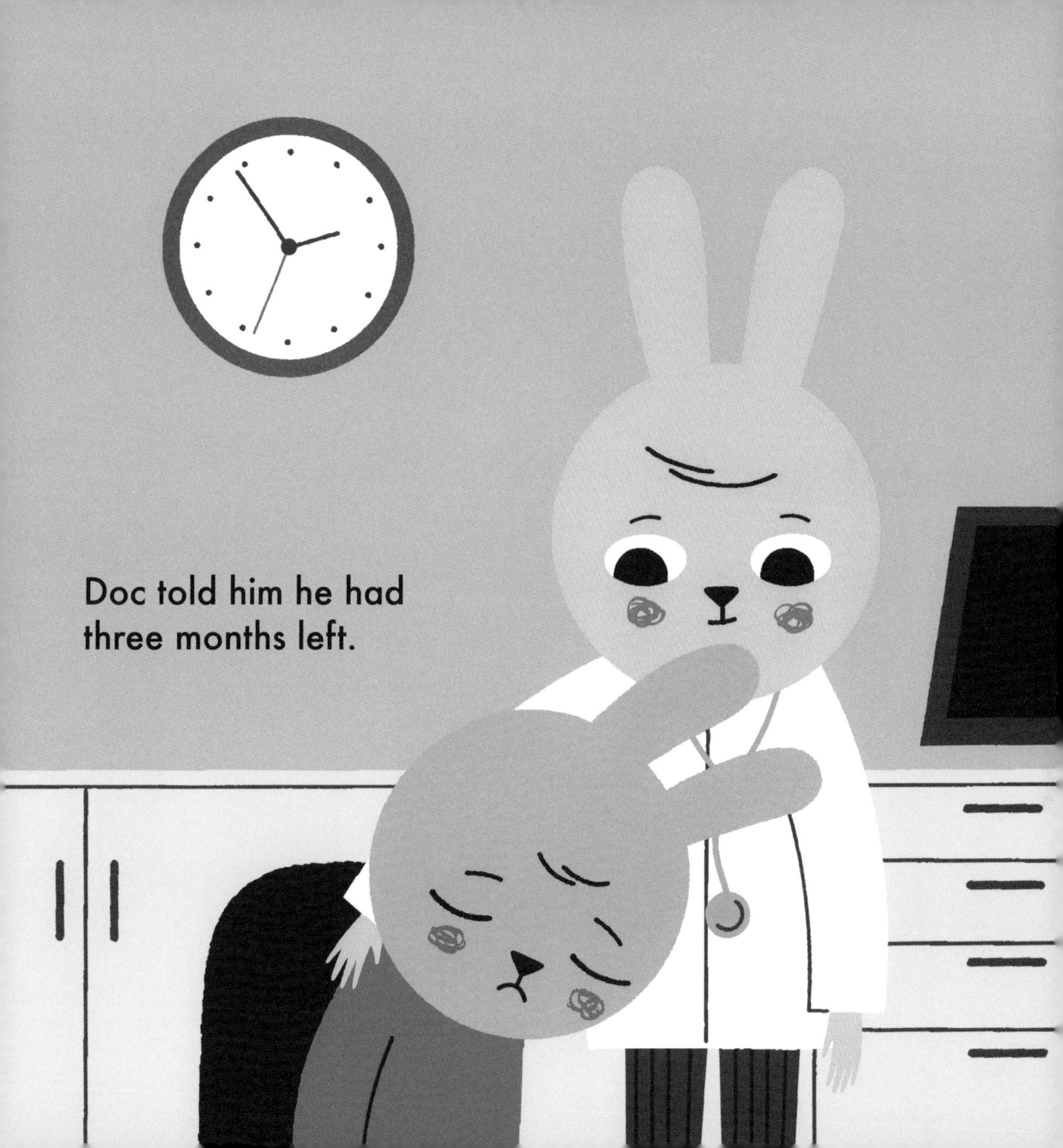

Doc told him he had
three months left.

Bunny was buried on a
sunny day in March.

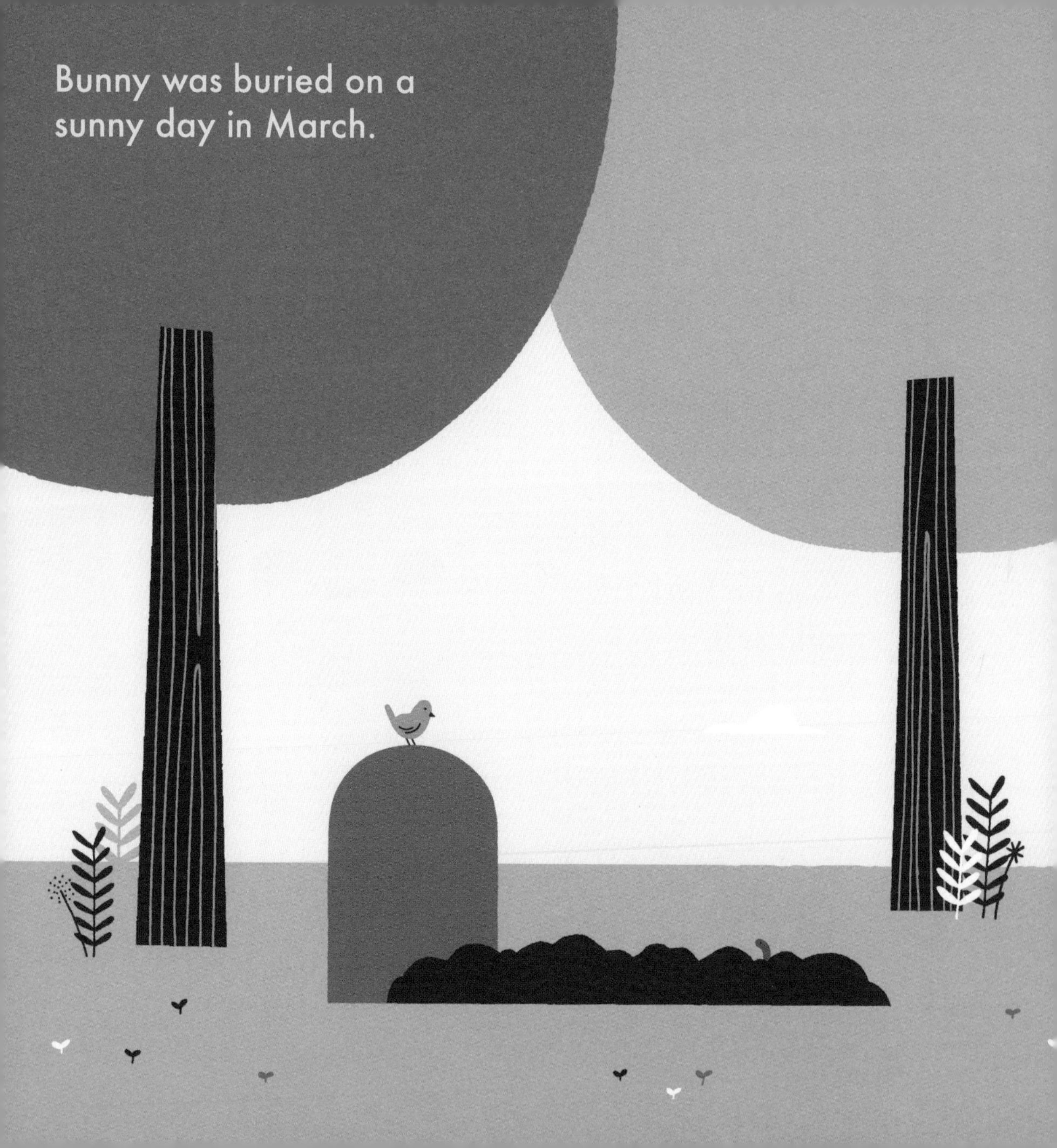

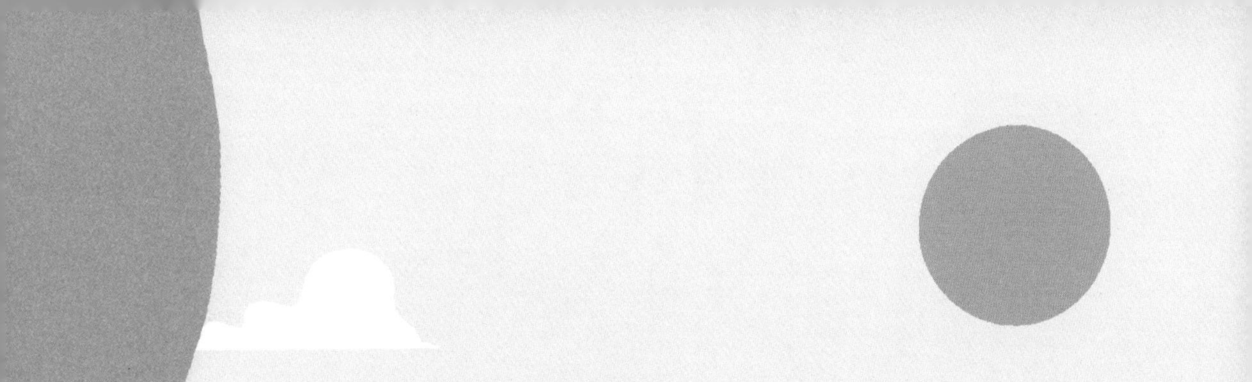

His life may seem grim. It wasn't really.
It just wasn't what we're taught to expect.

Maybe our expectations are rather too high – and so unwittingly rather cruel.

To be less surprised and saddened by life, to feel less alone, we might need to learn to tell one another slightly darker stories.

The kinds of stories Bunny would – almost – have wanted his children to read.

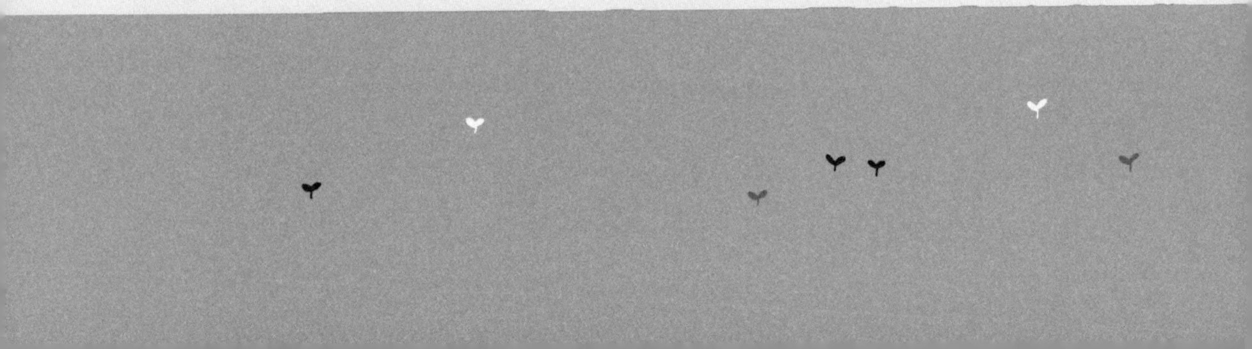

Published in 2017 by The School of Life
70 Marchmont Street, London, WC1N 1AB
Copyright © The School of Life 2017

Designed and typeset by Marcia Mihotich
Illustrations by Ben Javens
Printed in Latvia by Livonia Print

The School of Life offers programmes,
publications and services to assist modern
individuals in their quest to live more
engaged and meaningful lives. We've
also developed a collection of content-rich,
design-led retail products to promote
useful insights and ideas from culture.

www.theschooloflife.com

ISBN 978-0-9955736-8-0

10 9 8 7 6 5 4 3